Poetry collections from WritersCorps

PAINT ME LIKE I AM

TELL THE WORLD

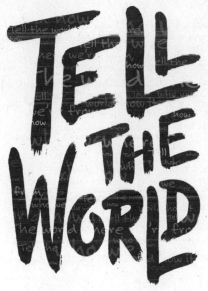

TELL THE WORLD

TEEN POEMS FROM WRITERSCORPS

Collins

HARPER TEEN

An Imprint of HarperCollins*Publishers*

Every attempt has been made to obtain release forms from the teens whose work is included in this volume. However, for those poets whose work is printed without a formal release, we do apologize for this omission.

HarperTeen and Collins are imprints of
HarperCollins Publishers.

Tell the World
Copyright © 2008 by WritersCorps
All rights reserved. Printed in the United States of America.
No part of this book may be used or reproduced in any manner
whatsoever without written permission except in the case of brief
quotations embodied in critical articles and reviews. For informa-
tion address HarperCollins Children's Books, a division of
HarperCollins Publishers, 1350 Avenue of the Americas, New
York, NY 10019. www.harperteen.com

Library of Congress Cataloging-in-Publication Data
    Tell the world : teen poems from WritersCorps. — 1st
HarperTeen ed.
        p.   cm.
    ISBN 978-0-06-134505-0
    1. Teenagers' writings, American. 2. Teenagers—Poetry.
I. WritersCorps.
PS591.T45T45 2008   2007049577
811'.60809283—dc22   CIP
                                                              AC

1 2 3 4 5 6 7 8 9 10
❖
First Edition

"A Poem," "Learning English Is Like," and "Anger & Poetry" from *Solid Ground.* © 2006 WritersCorps, San Francisco. Reprinted with permission from AUNT LUTE BOOKS.

"I Am," "Waiting," "When I Grow Up," and "How to Sing" from *City of One: Young Writers Speak to the World.* © 2004 WritersCorps, San Francisco. Reprinted with permission from AUNT LUTE BOOKS.

For the WritersCorps teaching artists who showed us the way

Contents

Foreword   xi
by Sherman Alexie

    A Poem

Tell the World Who We Are   3
    Wind over the Island of Cuba
    My Name Is Me
    Music
    Tea Cake
    Himalaya
    Who Am I?
    I, Too, Am an American
    Untitled
    I Am the Son
    Lightning
    I Am

Tell the World Where We're From   19
    Homesickness
    The House of Music
    Saturdays
    Where We Live

Prayer for the House
Waiting
Back in the Day
India
They Come From

Tell the World What We Love   37
A Collage
You Make Me Feel the Way I Feel
Voices of Wonder
My True Hero
Rules Are Simply
Devoted to the One I Love
Fading Love
Summer
On Love
Baby Sister
Untitled
So Much Alike
Lune
Watching God

Tell the World What We Think   57
Some Inspiration for the Reader
The One About
Proud Words

A Land of Our Own

Breathe

YOU and ME (also WE)

Haiku

His Chance

Middle-School Haiku

Questions Beyond Answers

So Much

Woman's Intuition

Ars Poetica

Why I Write

Tell the World How It Feels   83

Learning English Is Like

Sacred Wind

Loneliness

Haiku/Lune

Fear

Paradise

Struggles on Living in a Shelter

Spring and Autumn

Cycle of Life

I'm Fine

Who Am I?

Weather: Tornado

Sky Without Rain

Tell the World Why We Hope   99

    How To Sing

    I Dream

    For Spirit and Life

    Haiku

    Sunshine

    Untitled

    The House

    When I Grow Up

    Today

    God's Work

    Life

    Ride

    Anger & Poetry

WritersCorps History   119

Foreword
by Sherman Alexie

This introduction was difficult to write. It was months over-
due. I'm not sure why. I love the poems in this anthology. I
love their power, youth, and insight. But I guess I had a problem with that word: insight. Or rather, I had a problem with
its standard definition. I always have problems with standard
definitions. I don't want to be defined. Or rather, I want to
own a long list of definitions. I want an entire dictionary
page dedicated to my definitions. Two pages, ten pages, one
hundred pages. And I would guess the poets in this anthology
also want to resist the definitions assigned to them. The writers
seek to self-define, certainly, but I also think they admit to a
certain mystery, to the most basic mystery: Who am I? It's a
scary question, one that haunts all of us. It's a question asked
by our mirrors:

Near Sight

Something had irritated my left eye,
So I removed my glasses, and leaned close
To peer into my bathroom mirror and search
For an eyelash or mote of dust, but found

Nothing visible. With my terrible sight,

How could I've seen anything in my eye
Without my glasses? What I couldn't see hurt
Like crazy and I wondered if there was ground

Glass in my eye. But no, I would be blind
If that had been the thing. And then I glimpsed
A flash of feather, as if a small bird
Had crashed into my eye and spun around

To make a nest. No, that isn't the right
Simile. There's no need for simile
Or metaphor. I just need simple words.
With my left index finger, I pulled down

My left lid and leaned so close to the mirror
That my nose touched the glass, and was dumbstruck
To see an insect wing caught in the crevice
Between lens and lid. With my right index

Finger, I touched my eye, and hoped my tears
Would flood away the wing, but, no, it stayed
In place. I panicked and prayed. "Please, let this
Wing be one torn piece of a small insect

And not the entire monster." I feared
That a flock of houseflies had invaded

My eye. Or that a swarm of small locusts
Had turned me into food. O, I was wrecked

And ruined, but I found the courage to touch
The insect and pull it out of my eye.
It was just the wing, a part of the whole.
Relieved and joyous, I wanted to sing,

And realized I needed to construct
A Museum of Weird Stuff that People
Have Discovered in their Eyes. My first show
Will celebrate the painful insect wing,

Latticed and black, that scared the holy
Out of me, and the subsequent displays
Will feature daggers, bullets, and hot coals—
All of that painful and glamorous litter—

But it will also extol the common,
Like the pencil lead that I had to pull
Out of my eye after I tripped and fell
While walking and solving a crossword puzzle . . .

That's where I abandoned the poem. And that's where I abandoned my introduction to this anthology. Why did I freeze? I
don't know. But I sent that unfinished poem out to my friends

and they wrote back to offer advice, opinion, illumination, and, yes, insight:

1. This poem is about all the debris we collect inside us, some of it chilling, some of it rousing our mortality, pressing on our will to live, to see clearly, to remember/preserve.

2. Can't you ever write a normal email like: "How's it going? Nothing much. I got poked in the eye the other day." I read your poem to a couple of kids and they were awestruck. At least for a small period of time they stopped running around with pencils.

3. Your poem reminds me of the Romantics, especially Wordsworth and all of his "see see into the life of things" and the vision thing he got into where you penetrated something with your gaze alone . . . and isn't it Hopkins too? And the American transcendentalists with their transparent eyeballs? Maybe I'm mixing them all up here, but insight, foresight, sight-sight-sight is really something to work with . . . and the creature inside the speaker's eye, and then the feeling that maybe the person's whole head was infested . . . what comes in, what goes out, what gets in and stays there . . . there is something very spooky and haunting. And what happened to the rest of the creature?

Did only the wing get in or did the rest stay inside (somehow)?

4. There's definitely a strong relationship between your fingers and eyes, and your body being invaded through your vision. Maybe the bug who lost his wing in your eye was trying to send you a message. A message so urgent that he amputated his own wing to reach you. Like when you have dreams involving your eyes, they say it means there's something you refuse to see in your waking life. So you're accumulating a junkyard in your eyeball of things you refuse to look at in some regard . . . maybe?

What am I supposed to do with all of those opinions? Well, first of all, one can quickly realize that I have some genius friends who can read my poetry fragment and see the beauty and terror I could not. In writing about the insect wing I found in my eye, the wing that temporarily blinded me with tears, it seems that I was blind to its larger meanings, its poetic possibilities.

How often are we blind to our own possibilities? Often, I suppose. Always, perhaps. I realize that, in writing the poem about the insect in my eye, and my flawed vision, I needed my friends' eyes, their flawed visions, in order to have a chance at completion, at some fraction of understanding.

And, oh, yes, I need other people's poems to enhance my vision. I need the poems in this anthology to help me see:

Near Sight (2)

Child, I am an old man.
My eyes grow worse with each exam.
Take my hand, if you please,
Before I cross this dangerous street

In my dangerous city.
Ah, isn't every city a dangerous place?
Though I must ask:
What's more dangerous than a familiar face?

Child, let me borrow your eyes.
I want, I want, I want to be surprised
By the world. I want to renew my vows
With the endless, rushing crowds

In my dangerous city.
Ah, isn't every city a dangerous place?
Though I must ask:
What's more dangerous than a familiar face?

So, now, as I finish this anthology, as I shamble and stumble toward its conclusion, I can hear the slight music of insect wings. Are they flying toward my eyes? I don't know. But I can hear their songs, the music and lyrics, and just like the poems in this anthology, all of it is familiar, gorgeous, strange, and dangerous.

A Poem

is like a burning city
with dirty streets,
people
sleeping in the sewers,
rats
vanishing into tunnels.

Like putting the earth's core
into words
and making the poem
hesitate.

The streets are burning in fear.
The buildings are lit up by flames.

A poem

is putting the burning city
into words.

A poem is my firing mind
lighting up
with magical thoughts.

Rosy Mena, 13 *San Francisco, California*

Who We Are

Tell the World Who We Are

Who are you? Are you the child of the city you live in or the country you come from? Are you as steady as the beat of the music you love, as surprising as a bright flash of lightning, or as soothing as the sound of your grandmother's songs? Write a poem that shows through images that compare—metaphors and similes—who you are.

Wind over the Island of Cuba

I am the son of Cuba
where the ships are floating in Cienfuegos Bay
and the people are working hard
to survive their misery.
I am the son of the spring.
I am the beginning of everything
that makes things alive.

I am the son of the lion.
I have the strength to face the problems in this life
without any fear because my father protects me.

I am the son of the water.
My purpose is to satisfy the thirst
of the people who eat sand and darkness.
Many people seek me but they don't appreciate my flavor.

I am the son of San Francisco
where South Van Ness crosses Twenty-fourth Street,
where many people speak different languages.

I am the noise of the cars
and one old man selling ice cream,
and his voice sounds like a crow without hope.

I am history's child,
the wind over the Island of Cuba.

Dainiel Jimenez, 18 *San Francisco, California*

My Name Is Me

My name is strength
the strength in my legs I use to run up a hill

My name is wisdom
the wisdom I receive in the choices I make every day

My name is love
the love I feel when he looks at me

My name is pain
the pain that ran through my veins when my
    grandpa died

My name is independent
the independent person I became when my parents
    were sick

My name is power
the power that's in me to be who I am

My name is Me

Cynthia Rivera, 16 *San Francisco, California*

Music

I am Hip-Hop and R&B.
My mother is Old School.

I am Rap.
My grandmother is Smooth Jazz.

I am a CD that doesn't skip.
My grandmother is a broken old record player.

I am filled with music that will make you dance,
not just Hip-Hop, R&B, and Rap
but Reggae songs too, you know,
Daddy Yankee, Nina Sky,
Old School, New School, Go-Go.

I am all types of mixed songs
that other people can enjoy.

Danisha Simms, 13 *Washington, D.C.*

Tea Cake

i'm like a modern-day Tea Cake
my mom named me Michael Newby
but i'm better known as Prince Akzionz
smooth with his words as i am in composition
to top it all off both of us are musicians
live my life for the moment no set goals or missions
hip-hop complex young guys with free spirits
don't turn away from nothing we accept it as it happens
life on improv like freestyle rappin'
or freestyle actin'
but it's all reality no dvd on pause
the perfect man for Janey even in my flaws
when my words Hypnotize like Linda Jones
they say i hypnotize, but i'm not even into hypnotism
it's just me being me no silver tongue included
life on the edge and my love is deep rooted
and i do love some catfish
Janey on the other hand loves a man that takes a risk
let me tell you my daytime thoughts since you don't trust
    the night ones

Michael Newby, 17 *Washington, D.C.*

Himalaya

I am the green of your eyes
and the red tiny tomatoes
filled with the water of sadness.

I am the snow bear
skating on a frozen lake
and the Himalaya
shrinking day after day
and everyone knows why.

It's hard to say my name.
That's why people call me my nickname, Abdul.

I am the soccer ball who never
betrayed its team and offered them
the World Cup.

I am a young male red apple
feeding humanity,
an African of Moroccan blood,
fishing for the fourth language.

I am a giant cactus all alone
in the center of the ocean
protecting myself from the noise.

I am the end of the week
at school, the day of my favorite food,
couscous on the moon.

I am the blood of the Red Sea,
calm and warm.

Abdessalam Mansori, 15 *San Francisco, California*

Who Am I?

Who am I?
Am I a boy or a man?
Am I a thug or a G?
Am I Blood or a Crip?
I'll tell you what I am
I'm a quiet person who thinks a lot
I'm a person who wants to be somebody
Sometimes I might be a liar
Sometimes I might be a cheater
But all I know is that
I'm a person who respects you
I'm a person who will help you out
I'm a person who, if you cross me
Well, just don't cross me
This is me
This is what I see
And a good man is what I'm growing up to be
So don't try to stop or knock me
'Cause in the end no matter what you say
You're not me!

Shaquille Dorch, 13 *Bronx, New York*

I, Too, Am an American

I can be Chinese,
and not from China.
I say to them "I'm from the United States."
But others look at me and think I'm from Asia.
Even though I'm not from China,
I still speak that language at home with my family,
And celebrate Chinese holidays.
I can be American,
and not from America.
But the fact that I'm from here,
it's who I am!
America is and will always be my country.

I, too, am an American.

Untitled

Half Palestinian
Half Jew
What is this world coming to?
How did this happen?
How can I feel?
Dammit Mother! You never told
Now I feel so old
Growing I am.
Grown I'll be.
And one day this world will have a place for me.

Ilana Alazzeh, 14 *Washington, D.C.*

I Am the Son

I am the son of the fire
that burns the forest
that walks holding hands with the wind.

I am the son of Cobán,
where the language is beautiful,
the kids with dirty faces,
         torn clothes and old shoes.

I am the son of the desert
the sun strikes me,
the water falls and I drink all night,
and the snakes are my necklace.

I am the river that winds to the sea,
the lake my brother, the ocean my mom.

I am the son of thunder
that comes to the earth from the sky,
the lightning that breaks the rock.

David Barrientos, 14 *San Francisco, California*

Lightning

I am lightning
I crackle and I boom
Look at me, look at me
I branch across the sky
Like a giant fiery try
I stalk across the musty earth
On legs of crackling flame
I flash beneath the clouds
Brighter than the sun
But when the sun returns
The clouds carry me
Grumbling away.

Ramona Santana, 13 *Washington, D.C.*

I Am

I am the first spoken word of Swahili
that flowed like the river into Africa
I am the river that formed the mother and father of the
     world
I am the confidant of the king
the princess
daughter of Safria
I am the beauty of my land
I am the first fruit put into the basket on Kwanzaa
And there again the beautiful songs of
the spoken language
I am Aunt Jemima binding the family
I am Harriet Tubman
Dr. Martin Luther King freeing my people
I am the Black Panther in the souls of the righteous
     leaders
I am the June in Juneteenth
the celebration of my soul
I am the wild in the animals of Africa
I am the first African to set foot
on the moon
I am the inventor of all inventors
I am the future of my culture

Stephanie Dunlap, 19 *San Francisco, California*

Where We're From

Tell the World Where We're From

Where is your home? Is it the village you come from, or the city streets you walk every day? Is home where you smell your mother's chicken paprikash stewing on the stove, or where you hear your grandfather's laugh? Is home the feel of your favorite blanket, or the sight of your best friend smiling at you? Write a poem filled with the sensations—sight, sound, taste, touch, and smell—that mean home to you.

Homesickness

Let me become wind
to fly with the kite of childhood.

Let me become sunshine
to dance in my grandma's eyes.

Let me become chalk
to write with my teacher's hand.

Let me become a fish
to return to the ocean.

Let me become a wild horse
to run on the large highland.

Ngoc Minh Nguyen, 17 *San Francisco, California*

The House of Music

The house of music
    is where I live

When you walk
    it's like floating on a cloud
                filled
                    with soft bright music.

You would never have to walk
                as long as you have your music.

    The walls are made of piano keys.
    The walls are made of saxophones.

When it rains, the little raindrops
           turn into the brass

of the sweet saxophone
playing in the New York streets.

        My room is like my grandmother's hands
        holding me as tight as she can.

Dàvohntè Morgan, 15 *San Francisco, California*

Saturdays

the #30 bus on Stockton Street
stops suddenly
launches my sister and me forward
toward the crowded doors
we jump off the bus
dodging the elderly Chinese ladies
who walk slowly across the street
their backs hunched
hands burdened
with red plastic bags of fresh fish and ripe fruit

for an afternoon snack
I like to peel oranges
ripe flesh is easily torn away
the sticky sweet juice fills my mouth
clings to my fingers

my mother buys pineapple buns for lunch
they are plump and topped with a flaky golden crust
with only a slight resemblance to a pineapple's skin
crumbs fall into my lap as I eat

my sister and I run down the streets on Saturdays
on our way to dance class
mirrors echo us as we warm up at the barre
I suck in my tummy and stretch my legs
The chatter of girl giggles collapses
as we sink into the first position

I flail my arms like fluttering red fans
the way we leap up then hit the dusty floor
cracks like the snaps of children's firecrackers
striking the narrow sidewalks

real firecrackers burst through the sky
sparks flower into the night

what remains
wind pulls remnants of red paper
into the bakery's doors

Annie Yu, 18 *San Francisco, California*

Where We Live

where we live there are people with
loose lips that speak black words
found on street corners and gutters
their pale eyes stare directly at the
clasped hands that belong to you and me
the whispering begins before we've gotten
the chance to leave as their words
float before us in our faces causing
our skin to sweat.
let's run away from pairs
of pale eyes that disapprove
the sweet sensation
that flows from your fingertips
to mine, the love that embraces
the faults that we carry.
let's leave behind the heated
words that burn our skin
let's go to where our age is indifferent
to where judgment happens only
in the afterlife

Liana Castro, 17 *Washington, D.C.*

Prayer for the House

Peace unto this house, I pray
Keep terror and despair away
Shield it from evil and let sin
Never find lodging room within
May never in these walls be heard
The hateful or accusing word

Grant that love's warm and mellow light
May be to all a beacon bright
A flaming symbol that shall stir
The beating pulse of him or her
Who finds this door and seems to say

"Here ends the trials of the day"

Hold us together, gentle Lord
Who sits about this humble board
May we be spared the cruel fate
Of those whom hatreds separate
Here let love bind us fast, that we
May know the joys of unity

Lord this humble house we'd keep
Sweet with play and calm with sleep
Help us so that we may give
Beauty to the lives we live
Let thy love and thy grace
Shine upon our dwelling place

Maynor Gonzalez, 14 *Bronx, New York*

Waiting

I come from
a long line
of people who
divided the men
from the women.
I come from
a long line of darkness
and hate. I come from
a long line of people
who let their fear
take over. I come
from a long line
of no light.
I come from
a long line
of people where
you have to wait,
wait, and wait
to get what you want.
The line I am in
is the world
upside down.
I make a mistake,
and I start all over
again.

Robby Macam, 12 *San Francisco, California*

Back in the Day

Back in Birmingham, Alabama, there was segregation.
Black children couldn't get an education
And couldn't get treated with good medication.
When Rosa Parks protested she went to a police station.

Martin Luther King Jr. had determination
And with this, he affected the world, but especially
    this nation.
I never saw King alive but I'm thankful
for what he did for my generation.

Brittany Walker, 12 *Washington, D.C.*

India

India, why didn't you tell me
to stay in your arms?

Why are all the flowers in love
with each other?

Why didn't you come here
with me?

Why do you make me feel
like crying?

Why do you always tell me
what is good for me?

Why don't you understand
how difficult it is to stay alone?

Why can't I see you
from my window?

Why are you always there
for everyone?

Why don't you understand
how much I miss you?

Why don't you tell me a story
at night?

How can I tell you
how much I miss you?

Sandeep Kaur, 17 *San Francisco, California*

They Come From

by Michelle Matz, San Francisco WritersCorps teacher

They come from China, Korea, Egypt, Yemen, Mongolia. They left behind a dying mother who chose her daughter's education over her own medicine. They left behind wars and the scent of cherry blossoms. *I remember fall, leaves dancing down from the trees.* They arrive with a suitcase and an older brother. They live in cramped third floor walk-ups. They left behind *zongzi*, *pupusas*, *tamales*, rice dumplings. They come from El Salvador, Nicaragua, Russia, India, Cameroon. They speak Arabic, Mandarin, Vietnamese. They remember the weather the day they left their home. *The sun was still smiling and we were still cry-ing.* Their parents were doctors in Nicaragua and now clean office buildings. They take three buses to school. They left behind frail grandfathers. *I remember the smell of a flower opening up, a little sweet.* They speak Korean, French, Spanish, Tagalog. They come from Morocco, Chile, Eritrea, Haiti. They left behind the Yellow River, *a silk braid warming the earth.* Their fathers leave at five in the morning and return at eleven at night. They come from Vietnam, Thailand, Mexico, and Italy. *When you go away you become the rain falling silently to the river, the grass in the forest in need of sunshine, the dusty road.* They come alone, with a family friend's address scrawled on a piece of paper in their pocket. They befriend across oceans and continents, against tides and borders. They left moon festivals, red envelopes, rainy season. They come from Singapore, Hong Kong, Japan. *When my country says my name, it sounds like "come home."* They come documented. They come scared. They come undocumented. They left a war-torn country when they were infants. They had never left their small village until they came to America. *Let me become wind to fly with the kite of childhood.* They leave school early on Friday afternoon to attend mosque. They miss their friends. They miss the blue couch in the living room. *Family is like the harbor where ships can take a rest.* They remember what they ate for dinner the last night in their country. Their father lost an arm in the war. *Burma is water and I'm a flower.* Their mother leaves the apartment once a week on Thursday afternoon to buy vegetables at the corner market. They want to go home. *America is a mountain and I can't climb.* They hear gunshots from their bedroom window. They love Yao Ming. They miss their gardens. *I remember the smell of fresh air when rainy season is coming.* They come for better medical treatment for a younger sibling. They come for education. They come because they are hungry. They come because a neighbor's friend's uncle said it's better in America. They come to reunite. They come to separate. *My life feels like a flower but it is withered.* They left behind Tiananmen Square, Zhongshan Park, a stone forest. They left behind *Salatit Krumb, nam pla, kapee.* They live on 16th Street, 42nd Avenue, Mission Street. They miss walking along the Yangtze River with their grandfather. They come to school in America, sit in their assigned seats, write poetry about distance, loss. *Learning English is like drowning in the ocean.* Their words scatter across seas, sneak beneath doors in Bac Trung Bo, Moscow, Cairo, Guangdong. *I'm sorry to my old country. I'm sorry I can't stay in your hug.* I teach them vocabulary, explain metaphor, correct grammar. They tell me their stories. Stories about the taste of ripe mango, hiding beneath windows when the fighting started, how, in China, *the first quarter of the moon is a boat floating on the tranquil sea.* They ask me the meaning of words: homesick, winding, steel, gentle. They teach me to count in Mandarin, Thai, Russian. *Yī, nèung, adin.* They fall in love, write notes to each other on folded pieces of paper during math, play basketball in the school yard. They give me letters, photos, a blue-and-white knit scarf, bookmarks, origami flowers, earrings, a Chinese jacket. Our room is crowded, the rows of desks almost touching. The back window doesn't open. The side window doesn't close. Stacks of textbooks line the walls. There is no map in the room, no globe, no atlas. I bring a map from home, tape it to the back of the door. *I am an immigrant in*

America. I forgot to bring my soul here. I left her in my home-town. They point to their countries on the map—their cities, provinces, regions. They tell me how crowded their city was. They tell me they lived on a plot of land acres away from the nearest neighbor. They write poems to their countries. *Korea, why do you change your mind every season?* They write poems home.

What We Love

Tell the World What We Love

Who, what, and where do you love? Maybe you love your mother, boyfriend, or the kitten curled on your bed. Maybe you love summer evenings at the ballpark, or snow falling on Christmas. Write an ode—a poem of praise—about someone, something, or somewhere you love. Fill your poem with details: the hot chocolate your mother makes for you when you're sad, the way her walk is as fast as rushing spring water, the sound of her voice when she talks to your aunt on the phone, what she says when she's teasing, how her face looks when she's happy.

A Collage

For Chad Sweeney

The little mute girl was looking for her
Voice, in a drop of water.
Standing patiently, on the other side,
The dog grants the snow
A loaf of bread on his shoulders.
He said: The way is long,
But what you have,
Is this wave, snatched by the seagulls.
By the way, did you know that
A watermelon can heal in fifty ways?
The child was only listening,
Writing her own questions,
Clenching and opening one small hand.
You think I am speaking in riddles,
But the world only means itself.
There is nothing to throw away.
A proud voice later speaks:
I give to Chad a tulip
To thank him for teaching me
How to see.
To thank him for teaching me
How to build.

Indiana Pehlivanova, 16 *San Francisco, California*

You Make Me Feel the Way I Feel

You make me feel
Like an African Queen
Who doesn't have to lift a finger
You make me feel like a butterfly
Who is getting ready to burst out of her cocoon
To show off her beauty
Even though you are a woman who has been beaten
And didn't say anything because you were scared
Through all that you survived
You make me feel like an African Queen
You make me feel
The way I feel

Emauni Crawford, 12 *Bronx, New York*

Voices of Wonder

The lone Flower dreams as it listens
to the song sung by Flute,
accompanied by the echo of Trumpet
parading through the night as Cello
begins to move.

Sleep leaves the fountains and disturbs
the thirsty trees, hungering for the
touch of the collapsing bridge breaking
under the weight of the world.

The voice of Clarinet whispers a
song to the breezy morning,
waking those of the sleeping, ruffling,
the blankets and bed leaving them to wait
for you to return, allowing pillow
to recuperate from the weight being
lifted from its body.

The keys of Piano begin to leap with joy
as they exchange their love with Viola,
through their singing before the
eyes of hundreds, admiring their beautiful duet.

The voices of Cello soften
bringing darkness to a new level
as the requiem dies out completely
in voices of wonder.

Kitty Mei, 14 *San Francisco, California*

My True Hero

A hero is someone who stands up for
what they believe in and fights for what is right.
Some powerful heroes in the world that I know about,

heard about, or learned about in school are
Gandhi, Malcolm X, Martin Luther King Jr.,
Harriet Tubman, and Rosa Parks.

These are people who fought for what was right,
even when all odds were against them.
I think that defines a true hero.

I think of these people as heroes,
but none of them has had a direct impact on my life.
They weren't there to stop me from crying

When I fell off my bike and scraped my knee.
They weren't there to console me each time I
woke up in a cold sweat because someone was after me

and they surely don't make sure that I
eat every day and never go hungry and
that I always have clothes on my back.

There's just one person
who does all of this for me
and he is my true hero.

He is my dad.

Chea Sayon, 17 *San Francisco, California*

Rules Are Simply

rules are simply broken locks on open doors meant to
    be ignored,
written in a text that is easily erased and replaced.
let's walk thru those doors into a hidden world
of temporary ecstasy that envelops every dream
and desire we've never had the chance to achieve
let's taste the sweetness of the "should nots" and
"don't you evers" as we fulfill them
rules are simply ideas created by bland minds
that crave a softer touch than I possess
let's create a world where we can do as we please
where i can hold on to the clouds and jump from
rooftop to rooftop. let's talk in another language and
whisper sweet words that taste like caramel
when they fly from my tongue to your soul
let me kiss your fears as you grasp my
dreams with your bare hands.

Liana Castro, 17 *Washington, D.C.*

Devoted to the One I Love

You are as beautiful as the nighttime
Sky that shimmers with stars
Your beauty extends further than any
Stream of light

You are as precious to me as a cascade of jewels
On a mountain stream
You are more valuable than any diamond, ruby, or
emerald

You are as sweet as a lullaby sung by an angel
Your features are exquisite
Your skin is like music, a perfect harmony of tones
Put together to make something more
Beautiful than my words will ever describe

Angelica Amaya, 15 *Washington, D.C.*

Fading Love

My love for you is like
A marshmallow melting
Away.

My love for you is like
A raisin drying in the sun.
It fades when the sun is
Hiding in the night.

It fades and fades like
Chalk washing slowly off the
Sidewalk when it's raining.

Summer

Summer can be fun, summer can be great
You'll be eating pizza every night on a plate
Kids going outside playing in the water
Buying a soda that costs two quarters
Going in water having so much fun
Your eyes will be blinded by the sun
Kids going to the park, going in the pool
You better hope you don't go to summer school
Ice cream man comes around the block
Ice cream goes so fast it's out of stock
The sun is burning the kids are so hot
Sweating so much they just can't stop
Kids having fun playing with their toys
Older kids are playing with their Game Boys
Now summer's going away, going away fast
Soon summer will be a thought of the past
Fall is coming and the breeze is cool
Now the kids have to go back to school

Kenneth Mozee Jr., 14 *Bronx, New York*

On Love

you are sweet like a candy-apple lollipop
you are the wind, you help me breathe
you are a part of me and without you there's
no longer me, if ours were a fairy tale I would
like to be the shine in your armor and guard
you like an angel with love in my heart
when you're away from me you are on my
mind constantly

Amilcar Herrera, 14 *Washington, D.C.*

Baby Sister

Baby sister, I remember the first day you came home
     from the hospital,
Asleep on what used to be my favorite blanket;
Silent, looking like a black beautiful angel.

As the years went by I watched you get older and more
     beautiful every day.
Sometimes I get mad at you and think it's because I don't
     love you.
But I do with all my heart.

Now at four you're going to school,
And though you're getting older you're still going to be
     my little sister.
And I'll still love you.

Your Big Brother,
Jonathan

Jonathan Mewborn, 13 *Washington, D.C.*

Untitled

strong enough for a man
that's what mom would say. that true love is hard
to find. hearts and desires were felt to fall behind
who needs more than a man that cuts himself short
when a man says it's just not what it used to be
the other woman behind the glass door
set herself up for sure.
but as a woman waste not want not is
what you see, but i come easy as abc.
because i have long hair and brown eyes
should mean nothing to you.
because like, smart as i am, what a beautiful person
you really are. you get mad
when your friends say that safety is for sissies
but yet when we use safe sex we are not the
ones burning. the magical power of love
has set us free. the thought is that i can be
yours. we know the thicker, the better.
the smaller, the worse, cause the drama and
deep desire. that set your man up for sure.
a man that is the man of the house is my
shadow of love.

Krishawnda Smith, 16 *Washington, D.C.*

So Much Alike

You're skinny and sticklike;
I'm not so small.
I'm 5-feet-2 and you're so tall.
You'd love a jean jacket;
I'd like a nice white tee.
You'd pick up 50 pairs of jeans;
I'd pick the best 3.
You love to sit down and let the sun bathe your skin;
I run over to the pool and just jump right in.
You needed braces;
What a painful decision.
You also have glasses;
I've got 20/20 vision.
I have a little sister, you've got a little brother,
We laugh and promise not to let them fight with each
        other.
My birthday's January '92, yours is '91 December
We used to fight—you'd say you were the oldest,
Remember?
You would turn the heat down to 42
'Til your light-skinned face got pale and blue.
I'd turn the heat back up, stretch out
With you falling off the edge of the couch

And ignore your protests of "there ain't no space."
Well then, go sit some other place!
Change the channel! MTV's dumb.
You go outside and decide to "have fun."
I sit and watch you dance in the street
And slowly slip my shoes on my feet.
I join you as you sing what sounds to me
Like a rendition of "My Confessions" sung off-key.

Lune

Will our love
grow like an oak tree
will it, yes.

Shanda Gibbs, 16 *Washington, D.C.*

Watching God

every night i lay back watching my ceiling fan blades spin
50-degree breeze keeping me comfortable
maybe god is breathing on me from two directions
x-ray imagination let me see him thru my ceiling
dream so sweet it may lead to need for fill-ins
sometimes i lay next to janey starks when she was
    watching him
live from eatonville we broke the shackles of society
it's not expected of us, but we need it anyway
like swimming in my good clothes
like talking to the girl i love and drinking after her
like running off whole and coming back half
but on the other hand i look back to rebuilding

Michael Newby, 17 *Washington, D.C.*

What We Think

Tell the World What We Think

What do you think about the world that you live in? What do you think about school and the streets; about war and green gardens; about hope, faith, fear, and the future? Write a poem in which you say what you think. What voice will allow the poem to best share your thoughts? A loud voice, a sad voice, an uncertain voice, a proud voice? Speak your poem in that voice.

Some Inspiration for the Reader

What you write
Determines who you are
And what you get.

How you write it
Reveals what you want
And how badly you want it.

Whether or not you write
Determines how loud your voice is
And how far across the room your words will reach.

The One About

i can't give you that poem, the one about
love being the most valuable thing in the world
the poem with clever similes sprinkled through it
an ingenious rhyme for the word "cupid."

i can't give you that poem, the one about
a modern-day hamlet as soldier
and claudius as his corrupt general.

i can't give you that poem, the one about
a butterfly and its complex simplicity,
the one that makes me famous.

i can't give you that poem, the one about
the electric chair that washes up on the beach
the one that people misunderstand and
conclude that it's about overthrowing the government.

nevertheless
one of the attack dogs guarding the junkyard
has six puppies outside the gate.

Robin Black, 19 *San Francisco, California*

Proud Words

Proud words are like music blasting out of a stereo.

Proud words are like buffalos stampeding.

Proud words are like evil leprechauns stealing gold.

Proud words are like Miss Livia reading us poetry.

Proud words are hard to call back, like a bullet out of a gun.

Proud words are like Martin Luther King's "I Have a Dream" speech.

Proud words are proud words.

Proud words are friendships.

Proud words are powerful words, like asking someone to marry you.

Proud words are proud, and I just showed you mine.

Jonathan Mewborn, 13 *Washington, D.C.*

A Land of Our Own

This is the year
Norteños and Sureños put down their rags
and unite as one,
and lives will no longer be lost over a color.
Mothers will no longer stay up late
Worried over sons and daughters.
Words of wisdom
come from those
you least expect.

This is the year growling stomachs
full of pain and emptiness
feast on gold-plattered caviar
served by turned-up noses
dressed in rags.

This is the year everybody gets paid bread,
and minimum wage doubles.
This is the year
lower, middle, and upper classes
are considered equal.

This is the year Bush brings the troops home
and feels the pain he causes others.

This is the year
a president is sent to the front lines in Iraq,
left with a flooded house and living in a stadium
after Hurricane Katrina,
left in poverty by those he sentenced to death
through starvation.

This is the year people
who have been shot
or affected by a shooting
become healthy again.
The year Kong is able
to walk and see again.
This is the year Lil G's leg heals up
and he continues his basketball season.
This is the year my big homie
comes back to life.

This is the year he apologizes
for the last time and really means it.
This is the year she walks away
from the last punch he throws.

This is the year the grumpy old man
who sleeps on the grass gets to unlock the front door.
This is the year the staring woman staying in the box

is reunited with her family.
This is the year a homeless man wins the lottery.

This is the year the homeless
are gonna be able to buy a house;
the year they don't
have to eat out of the trash
but can eat in a fancy restaurant.

This is the year we can punch
the crooked cop in da chin.
No consequences, no arrests, but the cops
will feel it here.
This is the year I can run free without
the crooked cops looking down
at me.
This is the year that crooked cops will stop plottin'
but all their bad deeds won't be forgotten.
This is the year
crooked cops have no guns
and don't fight to be kool with
the teen in the hood.

This is the year
teens need to put them things down
for they ain't got to be six feet down.

This is the year Oakland murders will go down,
the year with no more teens buried underground.
This is the year
a mother or lil' brother don't
need to be scared that the oldest one
could be killed.

This is the year we put artillery away.
Everyone stand up if you wanna live to see another day!

This is the year
a father's fist
won't hit his child's face,
and the child will grow a voice
that surprises his father into a halt!

This is the year children will
grow wings and blow away any
harm in their path.

This is the year that abused children
will fly away to a land of their own.

This is the year.

Breathe

Breathe—
To start the
Inflation
Elevation
Soaring sensation
Levitation
Everlasting elation—
Until the sudden deflation.

Suzannah Fraker, 14 *Washington, D.C.*

YOU and ME (also WE)

Listen children . . . These are the ground rules.

Our parents are not home so **YOU** have to listen to **ME**.

YOU can't bother **ME** and **I** won't bother **YOU**.

YOU can't play with **ME** and **I** won't torture **YOU**.

YOU can't talk to **ME** and **I** can watch TV.

YOU can't ask **ME** for help with homework but

YOU can do whatever's legal and **I** can play on the
computer.

YOU can't cook and **I** can't either, so

YOU and **I** have to wait until our parents get home.

YOU and **I** are chemicals that don't mix because **I** am
baking soda and **YOU** are vinegar.

YOU stay in **YOUR** room and **I** stay in **MY** room.

When our parents come home **YOU** and **I** become **WE!**

68   **Lauren Chatman, 14** *Washington, D.C.*

Haiku

Too much destruction
In this world caused by violence.
Attacking the earth.

Edwin Flores, 13 *Washington, D.C.*

His Chance

It's hard to see someone you love not get that chance
The chance to be recognized for what he does
And not for how low he sags his pants and dips his hat
They label him as thug, murderer, drug dealer, or convict
But never father, companion, or genius
I question his future because I care
I question his whereabouts because I've been there
I been there since day one to see him on his knees
I was there on day two to see him get it together
And stand up on his own two feet
And say "I am a man, I am a man"
It's hard to see someone you know not get their chance
I know it's in him
I know he's got it
But they don't know
Because they never read between the lines of his real life
So do you think he has a lot of options?
I wouldn't say he does
So he does what it is that he does
He's a pharmacist, who delivers
He's a doctor who prescribes
And he's a sniper who hides out from all-seeing eyes
I am his eye, his right one at that

So before he crashes and his life is over
I'll give him a chance
To know that the way he lived is over
You don't have to live that life
Just as long as you know
That someone is out there
Giving you
A chance!

Romania Knight, 16 *Bronx, New York*

Middle-School Haiku

The sun sits gently
On a wide open landscape.
Waiting for the next.

The next day of life.
The life of Jaquan Clements.
What is my future?

More work and more rules.
Another difficult test.
Will I pass or fail?

Jaquan Clements, 13 *Washington, D.C.*

Questions Beyond Answers

Was there song before the birds?
Whistling before the wind?
Rustling before the leaves?
Did silence stretch across time like a vast plain,
Never ending and barren?
Or was there something before the beginning?

Who is more wicked,
The one who does evil,
Or the one who sees it being done and does nothing?
Should we blame all the witnesses of injustice,
Or just the culprits?

Who can change the thoughts of someone
Whose belief system is rooted in the ageless poetry and
    literature of faith?
How do you convince the unrighteous
That to serve God is to serve man?
And who can change an ageless misconception
In the minds of stubborn ignorants?

Who is to blame,
The mother for abandoning her child,

Or the father for taking advantage of the mother?
And who will save the innocents
When the worthy stop caring?

Sarah Verghese, 14 *Washington, D.C.*

So Much

Depends
On
A high school diploma
The gold ink
Shining
On
The paper
In my
Daddy's office.

Raiana Dos Anjos, 18 *San Francisco, California*

Woman's Intuition

Where you from?

What's that set you claim?

You gon rep it until death?

Or 'til the gunshots rang?

You gon love it even after yo right hand get slain?

Yeah it's fire in yo eyes but do you still feel pain?

You gon try a legal hustle or you gon jus sell Kane?

Boo you got knowledge past yo years

Why you don't use yo brain?

I guess you think cuz I'm a woman I ain't laced wit game?

You at an awkward disposition while you on the corner
      pitchin'

But baby boy is you 4getting that yo girl home alone
      wishin'?

And yo fate is in the distance servin' a long prison sentence

Because yo palms won't stop itchin' you gon be lyin' in a
      ditch

&

If you wonder how I know call it

Woman's intuition

Sharel Miller, 18 *San Francisco, California*

Ars Poetica

Poetry should be like a piece of sweet-potato pie
It should taste like broccoli with cheese and butter
It should sound like you really mean it
It should tell you what you want and what you need
Describe what you want it to sound like
Poetry should clear your chest and make you feel better
Poetry tells people how you feel so they can get to know
    you
And like you for who you are
Poems say stuff like her eyes are like the sky or
Her skin is like concrete
But it's supposed to clear your chest

Kionna McCurdy, 12 *Washington, D.C.*

Why I Write

by Beto Palomar, San Francisco WritersCorps teacher

I loved to read: the writing on the walls. As a kid I practiced decoding the gang scrawls that greeted me on my walks to school and back home. I knew these messages carried weight, maybe more than the lines of my school textbooks. I knew the lines on the walls meant there was a war going on outside and to be safe I had to understand their language. You learn to read the walls, you learn who is fighting who, and you have a better chance of avoiding the cross fire. Maybe that is why I felt a heavy urgency in my mind about words and language so early on.

School numbed my connection to language by making it routine and boring, stringing out words onto worksheets that reduced playing with language to a menial task, completing directions, following orders. For so long I was not interested in "literature," especially poetry—but somewhere inside me I had a deep respect for the power of words and language. I was aware, very early on in my life, of the distinctly separate worlds that some words existed in: immigrants and "native speakers," rich and poor. There was no intersection where the wild scrawls on the walls and the grammatically controlled and conservative lines of text that weighed a ton on our report cards crossed.

As much as I wanted to dismiss that academic world, I saw the powerful effect that intelligent words had on people, like teachers and cops who often assumed I was up to no good. I remember sharply the day I was snatched up by a school yard monitor who assumed I had started a fight I had suddenly found myself in. She grabbed me by the arm and marched me to the principal's office. I never spoke up, never told my side of the story, and I was made the criminal in that case. After that, I carried the pain of not having spoken up for myself.

I spoke up through graffiti. Me, the anonymous lost little mexicanito, meaningless, shuffled through the system, stuffed into the inner city, I wrote to proclaim my existence. Scrawling my name endlessly repeating like a Buddhist monk chanting a mantra of my own wild styling, I survived the gangster-thug-isms that claimed other youth around me. My homie Ruben went from As to Aks, but I just stayed sketching visions in calligraphy.

Through graffiti I continued to express myself and tried to develop my illustration skills. That led me to a teen youth organization called L.A. Youth that got me into illustrating for a newspaper that they distributed to L.A.U.S.D. students. The editor, knowing my passion for art and graffiti, asked me to describe my feelings about graffiti. That opened up a torrent of emotions and ideas and I wrote a piece that spiraled through my childhood and captured my ideas on the world around me at seventeen. I was, for the first time in my life, using writing to express something that really mattered to me.

I was trying to convince the world in that piece that I am not a real criminal. I am an artist shaped by his environment, which is in turn an environment shaped by other harsh realities of racism and classism. I was, for the first time, using words to defend my existence. After that experience I connected with writing. I was using writing to try to change the way people thought about graffiti, and the way they thought about me and those like me.

I got to see that writing was a powerful tool for change. Poetry, though, that was something else. It was a place where overeducated dead white men went to dazzle others with archaic annoying references and indecipherable abstract rambling. I saw poetry as a plaything for elites. It wasn't until I ran into the work of poet June Jordan, witnessing her students perform their own personal work at a poetry reading, that I began to know that poetry could also be powerfully used for real things. Poetry spoke to me that night, directly, about love and class and clash and beautiful and terrible things.

I joined that group of poets and studied with June Jordan and began to learn to use poetry as a form. I learned, most of all, that poetry should have a purpose. To me, and my writing, that purpose has always been survival. Criminalized because of skin and national origin, I always looked to writing as a place to stake myself out as a human, as a way to provide proof, concrete, absolute evidence of the fact that, yes, I am a full human being. Silly as that may seem, I'm always driven to describe how human I am, because so many things try to take that away. My goal now is to teach young brothers and sisters to wield words like handguns, and then ask them who the real criminal is.

How It Feels

Tell the World How It Feels

What emotions have you felt? Probably happiness, anger, loneliness, courage, joy, and dozens of others. Choose one emotion
and write a poem that personifies this feeling. Personification
allows you to write about something that isn't living, as if it
were a person. If happiness were a woman, what would she
wear? Where would courage live? What song would joy sing?
Who would anger hang out with?

Learning English Is Like

swimming in an ocean with many sharks
trying to see something when you are blind
walking on thorns without shoes
trying to hear something when you are deaf
staying in the sun without clothes for five hours
wanting to walk but not having legs
trying to type your schoolwork on a computer that
    doesn't have a keyboard
playing soccer without players
doing the English test without an explanation
going to the moon without a rocket
surviving somewhere that has no air
writing in a notebook that doesn't have pages
cutting paper without scissors
dancing without music
finding water in a desert
flying without wings
trying to see something in the darkness
seeing your boyfriend with another girl
standing in the rain without an umbrella
your house burning down
seeing a homeless person and not being able to help him

Luany Teles, 18 *San Francisco, California*

Sacred Wind

Freedom baby, come back to me
lift me off these hands and knees .
that I pray on every day.
Please, baby girl, don't let it be this way.
Fill these arms up once again
before loneliness becomes my only friend.
Missing your breeze so gracefully.
Freedom baby, come back to me.

Franklin Trieu, 18 *San Francisco, California*

Loneliness

Loneliness
lives in a single-room
apartment.
        Loneliness is just himself,
             and no one
             is with him.

He wears a plain white tee and blue jeans,
and a black jacket. He stares
off into the sky and thinks about what he has done
        in his life.

        Loneliness
        has many achievements and good grades
  but he is the only one to see them.
Loneliness has his own thoughts when being lonely.
He forgets that he is lonely with his friends
but only for a moment.

Loneliness exists in me.

Kevin Tran, 15 *San Francisco, California*

Haiku

Do you see my web
being destroyed by the broom
spider sadness, blooms.

Lune

I internalized depression
lock in my heart deep
have a key?

Tony Bush, 16 *Washington, D.C.*

Fear

Fear lives in a busy city,
In the projects, with broken windows
Spiderwebs on the doors, walls, and
Floors. Fear wears a gray baggy coat,
And a jumpsuit too big for his size. He tries
Too hard to fit in with the cool group but just
Can't. The sound of fear is trembly and out of place.
Fear's mother died when he was two years of age. But
He only heard rumors of her. Fear's father left when he was
A baby. They were finally reunited, but Fear's father
    pulled his hair,
Cursed at him, and lied to him, trying to make everyone
    else look
Bad. Fear's biggest fear was turning into his dad. All fear
    wanted was
    To be normal, to live a normal life.

Michael McElroy, 14 *San Francisco, California*

Paradise

There are no white beaches here.
No beautiful sparkling waters.
This is not what you think it is.
This is paradise.

The sun never rises.
The moon never sets.

The sea is an everlasting puddle
Of black ink.
Within its inky depths are the souls
Of a thousand lost men.

Smiles melt off the faces
Of the fortunate.
The lost and the distressed
Are in my good graces.

It's dark in my paradise.
The stars glitter in the sky.
They are the only lights I see.

Ariana Faunteroy, 14 *Washington, D.C.*

Struggles on Living in a Shelter

My life is something that I don't like to live
It's something I cry about every day
It makes me feel like I am nothing
'Cause when I go to school
I know I have to come back to a shelter
Sometimes I am like, damn, my mom can't find an
    apartment
Many times when I am at school
My friends want to know where I live
But I am too ashamed to say
Now it's like, whatever, because I know when I grow up
I will not put my kids through the stress my mom put
    me through
'Cause I'm going to win
And a nice big house
Is where my life will end

Shekuanzie Dorch, 12 *Bronx, New York*

Spring and Autumn

I sit big and tall
On the smooth bark of a
Wonderful maple tree
Beautiful birds
Soar over me
Every ten minutes
I hear dogs barking
Cats purring
I melt every time
Someone lays a
Finger on me

I dry up like
Corn bread batter
That's been sitting
Out for days
I crackle as if I was
On fire
I get really cold and
Start to break off my bark
Turn and turn
In circles until
I hit the ground

Nicole Williams, 17 *San Francisco, California*

Cycle of Life

The moon is a mirror.

The mirror is a song,

Words filled with sadness.

Sadness is my life,

But also my addiction.

My addiction is a curse

Seared into my body and soul.

My soul is gone

Leaving a monster.

This monster is I.

I am a butterfly.

The butterfly is a balloon

Rising to the moon.

Joanne Ko, 14 *San Francisco, California*

I'm Fine

I bleed away my problems
I scratch them all away
My problems drip away from me
And slither down the drain
My problems are dissolved in crimson
My scarlet poison makes them die
A piece of metal shatters them
And through my veins the pieces fly
These scars upon my skin
Tell tales of secret pain
But come and listen to them
Of the truth I'm not ashamed
My problems are hidden from you
I hide them oh so well
What's wrong?
I tell you nothing
You can't save me from this hell
I'm fine

Maynor Gonzalez, 14 *Bronx, New York*

Who Am I?

I came out of this rounded earth that I made.
I put those glowing things in the sky at night.
My breath is the wind that makes you cold.
When I cry I give you rain.
Thunder comes from my anger.

I can climb to the sky
to make fluffy pillows
tell the sun to shine on you.
I can come back down
without salty water dripping from my skin.

I have diamond trees
in my backyard.
I gave my mother
the gift of Venus
the planet I named after her.

I can burn you
like an ant under a magnifying glass
the hot sun searing it.
I can catch a star
like the fisherman tosses his pole into the sea.
I fold this earth
like a mother folds laundry.

Tina Hu, 17 *San Francisco, California*

Weather: Tornado

A tornado.
Look at it, and what do you see?
Life itself.

Folded within the layers
Of the swirling vortex
I believe there is a soul.

Smell the earth around you,
Inhale the beauty.

First there are problems and obstacles,
Then all is still and quiet.
You turn around again
And there's another tornado.

Ariana Faunteroy, 14 *Washington, D.C.*

Sky Without Rain

Without you
  I am a tree without leaves,
a rose
without petals.

Without you
  I am a heart without life,
and a sky that cries
without rain.

Without you
  I am a garden without flowers,
a river
without water.

Without you I am a road without end.

Ana Madrigal, 16 *San Francisco, California*

Why We Hope

Tell the World Why We Hope

What hopes do you hold in your heart or your head? Write a poem that uses alliteration: the repetition of the starting sound of many words in a line. Do your dreams drum or dance? Is your family's future fabulous and full of fun? Are your wishes weak, watery waltzes, or wide, high-wattage welcoming whales?

How To Sing

First, you have to open your mouth
so you can let out a song
that will make the birds jealous enough
to crack the sky.

Make the song so beautiful
angels cry.

Sing 'til church bells ring.
Sing from the heart.
Sing, baby, sing.

Dannesha Nash, 12 *San Francisco, California*

/ Dream

of Paris in springtime
to find each person
before the night sky/opened-up heaven with livid walls
ancestral gold eagle descended before me
desire to live/write dream love travel crash wake bleed
    dance
imbued within my soul
drink in time with no time at all/the cadence of time
can kill time in a flash
the inherent density of man's addiction/a beautiful yellow
    can
tumbles like a fifty-pound rock
like death on fire/air will no longer be angel blue

Samson Lei, 18 *San Francisco, California*

For Spirit and Life

Right now, a grandmother is making tamales for dinner
And a man and woman are kissing at the park.

Somewhere two animals are running for their lives,
  Somewhere a lion is eating a gazelle.

At this moment a tree is breathing fresh air.
At this moment a river is running, giving fresh water
To a village in Australia.

At this moment an eagle is flying freedom.

Right now a soccer game is starting,
  An ambulance is rushing to the hospital.

At this exact moment some kids are watching *Teletubbies*.
At this exact moment some kids are sleeping.

Right now in the world many people are working
  And fighting for their lives and their families' lives.

Somewhere it is very hot, and the people are thirsty
For spirit and life. Somewhere a tree is being cut.

Right now a whale is swimming,
    A fish is trying to escape from an octopus.

Someone is helping a woman at the hospital
So she doesn't die.
    Someone is drawing a picture of Jesus.

En este momento mi tío, mas joven que yo,
    Está en la escuela, haciendo su trabajo.

En este momento! Right now! Right now!

Francisco Figueroa, 15 *San Francisco, California*

Haiku

As I walked the beach
the cold water at my feet
the moon smiled at me.

Shanda Gibbs, 16 *Washington, D.C.*

Sunshine

summer makes me happy
sunshine makes me run
on the beach I play and build
sand castles and then I swim
in the ocean where dolphins
jump the waves with me

when the sun sets
and the moon comes up
the wolves howl at the night
I am scared in my bed alone
so I think of songs that make
me happy and I sing
until I fall asleep

Cong Nguyen, 13 *Washington, D.C.*

Untitled

My brain has the knowledge I need to hold
My mouth tells all the stories I have foretold
My hands can massage all fears away
In my arms is where I want you to stay
I walk with a pace of grace and style
Holding my head up high with a beautiful smile
My legs strong and powerful when I walk
A soft and soothing voice when I talk
In my head I am a phenomenal young lady
Never will I say about myself: *Maybe*.

Shanda Gibbs, 16 *Washington, D.C.*

The House

I am making a house
With my mind full of
Fantasy.
I am building a house with doors
Of shiny diamonds
To amaze my eyes.
There is a special place
For my baby to play in a colorful garden
And she will look like a wonderful
Orchid from my garden.

Music comes from the sounds of the wind
The sounds of the birds
The sounds of the waves of the sea.

I'm building a house with love
Building a house with hope
Where all the good people are welcome
A house that moves my enemies away from me.

The house has a magic bedroom
Where, when I sleep,
I can see above my bed a dark sky with many stars.

Beautiful curtains open
To show me the rays of the sun
When I'm happy.

Karen Blanco, 14 *San Francisco, California*

When I Grow Up

When I grow up, I want to remember
how much I loved to tie my short hair
with a beautiful ribbon,
or tear off the paper of the calendar,
how scared I was of ants that crawled toward me slowly,
how much I hated that the babysitter asked me to sleep
when I was full of vitality,
what fun it was to draw pictures on the wall with
     crayons,
to fold a paper airplane and fly it.

Yan Jun Xu, 15 *San Francisco, California*

Today

Today is my future.

With knowledge and education,

I care more about my future success, about my family's
  future.

My heart now has a list of things that must be completed.

I have my head up staring at my destiny that is so close
  yet just out of reach.

I see my career that will put bread on my family's table,
  more friends that will guide me through life,

And I will write poems about the whole adventure.

Now all I have to do is make my destiny, as I see it, come
  true!

That's what must happen, because I can't live in poverty
  anymore.

That's why I can't wait until tomorrow because,

Today is my future!

Marisol Rodriguez, 13 *Bronx, New York*

God's Work

The sea and water
form what I see.
The stars and the moon
glance back at me.
The wind blows through
the trees, wide and free.
And then come the engines
loud as can be.
Lights blast orange
and wild.

Markeeta Knight, 14 *Washington, D.C.*

Life

Life is like a coin you can only spend once.
To some it is a challenge, a battle to stay alive; to others
it is beautiful and silky fine . . .

Life is a journey, a journey in which we love, we hate, we
suffer but in the end you know you have to deal
with the struggles.

Life is a conquest that can be explored at any time and in
any way.
To some, life is like the ocean full of conflict, full of pain,
it is like thunder when it's cold outside, a fire burning
when it rains.
But life can only be lived once.
To live life to the fullest is the way to go.
To enjoy every moment and know nothing can bring
you down.
To wake up every morning and say, "I'm still alive."
That's truly the journey of life.

Luis Nieves, 15 *Bronx, New York*

Ride

Over my shoulder I see it rise,
This is it, the one, the only one,
I flatten and paddle, harder,
Harder, and my arms get numb,
I rise with the wave,

I spring to my feet, I swerve to the side,
The crumpling wave beneath
Shoots me forward like a winter wind,
I reach the hard dry sand,
And go out to do it again.

Porter Ryan, 14 *Washington, D.C.*

Anger & Poetry

Anger is like breaking
all the plates
and ripping out
the windows.

Poetry is like seeing
the whole world.

Alma Garcia, 12 *San Francisco, California*

WritersCorps History

WritersCorps is a celebrated national arts and literacy program. Each year, in three cities, hundreds of young people—often living in some of the nation's most economically disadvantaged neighborhoods, youth whose voices are systematically ignored or disregarded—experience firsthand the power of writing about their lives, thoughts, observations, and dreams. The accomplished writers who serve as WritersCorps teaching artists create innovative lessons that make literature relevant to the young people they work with, and offer respectful relationships that give the ground of support that youth need. Award-winning publications and popular reading series provide means for young writers to share with the larger community.

WritersCorps was born out of discussions between Jane Alexander, former Chair of the National Endowment for the Arts (NEA), and Eli Siegel, then-director of AmeriCorps. San Francisco, Washington, D.C., and the Bronx, N.Y., were selected as the three initial sites for WritersCorps, chosen for these cities' exemplary art agencies with deep community roots and for their traditions of community activism among writers. Since 1994, WritersCorps teaching artists, working at public schools and social service organizations, have helped young people of virtually every race, ethnicity, and age improve their literacy and communication skills, while offering creative expression as an alternative to violence, truancy, alcohol, and drug abuse.

In 1997, WritersCorps transitioned from a federally funded program to an independent alliance, supported by a collaboration of public and private partners. DC WritersCorps, Inc. is now a nonprofit organization, while the San Francisco and Bronx WritersCorps are projects of the San Francisco Arts Commission and the Bronx Council for the Arts, respectively. WritersCorps has developed a national structure administered by these three sites to provide greater cooperation and visibility, while at the same time allowing the independence for each site to respond most effectively to its community.

To learn more about WritersCorps contact:
Bronx WritersCorps: 718-409-1265 or www.bronxarts.org
DC WritersCorps: 202-332-5455 or www.dcwriterscorps.org
San Francisco WritersCorps: 415-252-4655 or
www.writerscorps.org